OUT OF THE DEPTHS

OUT OF THE DEPTHS

——◆——

Restoring Fellowship with God

D. MARTYN LLOYD-JONES

This book contains the substance of four sermons
preached at Westminster Chapel, London,
in October 1949, and subsequently published
in the June-August 1950 issues of
The Westminster Record.

Out of the Depths

© Elizabeth Catherwood, 1995

First published 1987 by Evangelical Press of Wales

This edition is published by special arrangement with
the Evangelical Press of Wales, Wales, U.K.

Published by Crossway Books
        a division of Good News Publishers
        1300 Crescent Street
        Wheaton, Illinois 60187

Cover design: Cindy Kiple

First U.S. printing 1995

Printed in the United States of America

ISBN 0-89107-838-X

Library of Congress Cataloging-in-Publication Data
Lloyd-Jones, David Martyn
    Out of the depths: restoring fellowship with God / David Martyn
Lloyd-Jones.
        p.   cm.
    1. Bible O.T. Psalms, LI—Criticism, interpretation, ect.
2. Repentance—Biblical teaching.   I. Title.
BS1450 51st .L55 1995   223'.206—dc20   94-33867
ISBN 0-89107838-X

03	02	01	00	99	98	97	96	95
15	14	13	12	11	10	9	8	7	6	5	4	3	2	1

CONTENTS

PUBLISHER'S FOREWORD

Sin—it is not a word that the modern world likes to talk about. Yet for all our attempts to pretend that it doesn't exist, sin won't go away. The morning headlines remind us everyday. But there is an even more persistent reminder—whenever we stop to reflect on our own thoughts and actions.

As Dr. Martyn Lloyd-Jones saw so clearly, "We have all sinned against God. We can never get rid of our guilt, we can never remove the stain. My past remains and I cannot deal with it, and I fail in the present and shall fail in the future." How can I ever find peace and rest and relief from the guilt that will not go away?!

For the answer to this question, Dr. Lloyd-Jones turns to Psalm 51, the classic statement on repentance and forgiveness in Scripture. Lloyd-Jones shows first that each of us must recognize the terrible reality of what sin actually is; and that even though we may never have committed the "big sins," we are still sinners and utterly helpless apart from God's solution!

———◆———

But there is an answer—an answer provided by God Himself to pay the penalty for our sins, to wash away the indelible stain of guilt, to enable us to live victoriously in the midst of a sin-plagued world. What we cannot do for ourselves, God has accomplished for us—by grace through faith— that we should know the joy of our salvation. As Lloyd-Jones explains, the wonderful truth is that "the gospel does not just forgive you and urge you to go back and live a better life. It gives [you] a new life."

This classic study offers a rare and profound understanding of the meaning of salvation—offering the assurance that our sins have been forgiven once and for all through the blood of Christ, but equally that we may the love and compassion and mercy of God as we walk with Him day-by-day.

For those who do not know of Dr. Martyn Lloyd-Jones, he has often been referred to as one of the greatest preachers of this century. He is noted for his penetrating diagnosis of the human condition, and for his persuasive proclamation of the gospel as the only sufficient answer. Dr. Lloyd-Jones served as the pastor of Westminster Chapel, London, until 1968, and continued to preach throughout Britain until his death in 1981. Prior to entering the ministry, first in Wales and then at Westminster Chapel, he was a distinguished medical doctor. Early in his career, however, he left the

———◆———

medical profession to pursue a higher calling, namely the "cure of souls."

We are grateful to Dr. Lloyd-Jones's heirs and to the Evangelical Movement of Wales for the opportunity to publish this new edition here in North America.

> Lane T. Dennis, Ph.D.
> President, Crossway Books
> September, 1994

Psalm 51:1-5

'Have mercy upon me, O God,
according to thy lovingkindness: according unto
the multitude of thy tender mercies blot out
my transgressions. Wash me throughly from
mine iniquity, and cleanse me from my sin.
For I acknowledge my transgressions: and my sin
is ever before me. Against thee, thee only,
have I sinned, and done this evil in thy sight:
that thou mightest be justified when thou speakest,
and be clear when thou judgest. Behold,
I was shapen in iniquity; and in sin did my
mother conceive me'.

I

THE SINNER'S CONFESSION

◆

Psalm 51:1-5

It is generally agreed that this fifty-first psalm is perhaps the classic statement in the Old Testament on the question of repentance. Indeed, there is a sense in which it can be said that it is perhaps the classic statement on this whole matter of repentance in the entire Bible. It is the record of the agony of soul of David the king of Israel after he had been guilty of a particularly dastardly crime. A little caption in the Authorized Version says, 'To the chief Musician, A Psalm of David, when Nathan the prophet came unto him, after he had gone in to Bath-sheba.' In other words, there is a sense in which we cannot truly understand this psalm and

◆

its teaching unless we bear in mind the background which led to it.

It is a very unpleasant story. Yet I must remind you of it because life can be unpleasant. We are all, alas, capable of doing unpleasant things. The story in its essence is this. David was the king of Israel, and at this particular point in his reign his armies were engaged in warfare. David himself was not with the army; he had remained behind in Jerusalem. We are told that one day he happened to be seated on the roof of his house looking, apparently accidentally, in the distance, when he saw a very beautiful woman. This woman was the wife of a man who was fighting with David's armies against the foe. David, having looked, and having liked this woman, coveted her and commanded her to be brought to him. She was brought to him and he committed adultery with her. He defiled her. Then, to cover up his sin, he sent to his commander-in-chief, Joab, and told him to send home Uriah the Hittite, the husband of this woman. He came and had an interview with the king. The king then dismissed him and told him to go home.

But this man was a man of honour and he did not go home to his wife. He felt he should not do that when the king's armies were on the field of battle and when perhaps the fate of Israel was in jeopardy. He said, 'No, no! . . . I cannot do that,' and he slept on the doorstep. The king heard of this and he

◆

made the poor man drunk in an attempt to send him home. But again Uriah refused. So David wrote a letter to Joab and sent it by the hand of Uriah. He said, in effect, 'I want to get rid of this man; you must somehow or other put him in the forefront of the battle.' Joab carried out the command. He arranged that Uriah the Hittite, and certain others, should be put in the forefront of the battle where the most valiant men of the opposing army were to be found. Poor Uriah was killed. Thus David obtained what he wanted and had his satisfaction and took this woman, Bathsheba the wife of Uriah, to be one of his wives. All seemed perfectly well. 'But the thing that David had done displeased the Lord' (2 Samuel 11:27).

David, however, went on quite happily until God sent Nathan the prophet to him. Nathan said to the king: 'I have rather a sad thing to report to you. There were two men in your kingdom; one was a wealthy man and he had great flocks and an abundance of sheep and oxen, and there was another man, a very poor man who had just one ewe lamb. It was a kind of pet with him. But it happened that when somebody paid a visit to the great rich man, instead of killing one of his own sheep he took the one ewe lamb of the poor man and killed and dressed it for his guest. The poor owner was broken-hearted.' David arose in wrath and declared: 'The man who has done such a dastardly thing must be punished immediately!' Nathan then stopped him and said, *'Thou* art the man!', indicating that he had been speaking a parable to him to remind and to point out to him the very thing he himself had done in the case of Uriah the Hittite. That is the background.

David suddenly sees it and is filled with a sense of shame and horror, and it was in that condition that he wrote this fifty-first psalm. There is the story, there is the background. Now I hope to study this psalm with you because it directs our attention in a very graphic and forcible manner to some of the basic truths and facts concerning our life in this world. It especially bears on the great matter of our salvation.

According to the Bible there are certain steps through which we must of necessity pass before we can know the salvation of God in Jesus Christ. We go to church Sunday by Sunday because we are concerned about the propagation of the gospel of our Lord Jesus Christ. My only reason for standing in the pulpit is that I believe that here in this Book is contained God's way of salvation for mankind. It is the one thing that the world needs today. It is the answer to man's need, and yet men and women ignore and deride it. There are many who are interested in it, and yet they have not experienced its power and saving grace. Why? Well, I say simply, it is because they have not realized that there are certain things which must happen before a man can experience the great salvation which is to be found in this gospel. There are certain things that we must realize, we must grasp, we must believe, and the first of these is repentance. That is why we are starting with this psalm; we must be clear about the whole question of repentance.

Read the case of any convert you can find in the Bible and you will always find that this element of repentance comes in. Read the lives of the saints, read the history of men who figure in the church of God in past ages, and you will find that every man who has really known the experience and the power of the grace of God in his life is always a man who gives evidence of repentance. I do not hesitate, therefore, to make this assertion, that without repentance there is no salvation. The need for repentance is one of those absolutes about which the Bible does not argue. It just says it. It just postulates it. It is impossible, I say, for a man to be a Christian without repentance; no man can experience the Christian salvation unless he knows what it is to repent. Therefore I am emphasizing that this is a very vital matter. John the Baptist when he began his ministry went out and preached the baptism of repentance for the remission of sins. It was the first message of the first preacher. Our Lord and Saviour Jesus Christ, we are told by Mark, went about and preached that men must repent. Repentance is *absolutely vital*. Paul went about and preached repentance towards God and faith in our Lord Jesus Christ. Peter preached on the day of Pentecost the first sermon under the auspices of the Christian church, and when he had finished certain people cried out, saying, 'What shall we do?' 'Repent!' said Peter. Without repentance there is no knowledge of salvation, there is no experience of salvation. It is an essential step. It is the first step.

'Very well,' says someone, 'what do you mean when you say we must repent?' Now this psalm is a classic statement on the whole matter and doctrine of repentance. In this first study I only want to deal with one aspect and one step, with what I regard as the first step in repentance. It is conviction of sin, or, if you like, it is our confession of our sinfulness. If you care to give a title to this sermon, you could say that we are going to deal with the sinner's confession, our conviction of sin and the confession of our sinfulness.

Here, again, is something that I do not hesitate to describe as an absolute essential. It is because they do not realize the biblical teaching concerning sin that men fail to realize so many other things that are contained in the Christian gospel. There are so many people today who say that they do not see the need of the incarnation; that they do not understand all this talk about the

Son of God having come down to earth; that they do not understand this talk about the miracles and the supernatural; that they cannot follow this idea of the atonement and terms such as justification and sanctification and the rebirth. They say that they do not understand why all this seems to be necessary. They would argue like this: 'Isn't it the church that has evolved all these theoretical, purely abstract ideas? Aren't they things which have been conjured up in the minds of theologians? What have they to do with us, and where is their practical relevance?' I would like to point out that people who talk like this do so because they have not realized the truth about sin. They have not realized the full meaning of the biblical teaching about sin. They have not realized that they themselves are sinful. But the Bible, in sharp contrast, constantly insists upon this from the beginning to the end. Indeed, I would put the Bible's challenge to the modern world in this form. It tells us that the life of man, whether individually or collectively, simply cannot be understood apart from the doctrine of sin. Here we are in this modern and perplexing world; we are conscious that something is wrong, and the question is: 'What is wrong?' Politicians do not seem to be able to solve our problems. Philosophers are asking questions but they do not seem to be able to answer them. All our efforts do not seem to put the world right. The Bible

◆

says, 'You are ignoring the one thing which is the key to the situation! It is sin. Here is the cause of the trouble in individuals, in intimate human relationships, in international relationships everywhere. This is the difficulty.'

Now the Bible emphasizes this everywhere and in an amazingly honest manner. That is to me always one of the most extraordinary, fascinating things about this Book. It conceals nothing. I cannot understand the man who does not believe in this Book as the Book of God. It is so very honest. It does not attempt to whitewash its greatest heroes. It does not attempt to build up a great picture of a collection of heroes without blemish. Mythology does that and mankind generally does it. But the Bible never does so. It shows men in their weakness as well as in their strength. It does so for one reason only—its ultimate interest is not in these men at all, but in the truth of God. I want you to see that the common idea that Christians claim that they are better than other people is an utter travesty of the Christian position. The Christian position is rather that I believe that I am utterly and absolutely hopeless apart from the grace of God. I am what I am by the grace of God— that is the biblical statement. The case of the Bible is that the only hope for man is in the gospel and in the grace of God. This is a gospel for sinners. There is a sense in which it has nothing to say to a man until he sees himself a sinner. In other words, the object of its statements to him is to make him see himself a sinner. The Bible has nothing to say to a man who has not repented. Its first call is a call to repentance. In this way does it deal with this terrible doctrine of sin.

And its case about sin can be put in this form, that sin is a terrible malign power, that sin is such a terrible, such a powerful thing that it gets us all down, that every man who has ever lived in this world has become the victim of it. It tells us that the power of sin is as great and terrible as this— that even a marvellous and wonderful man like David the king of Israel could fall in the way I have already described. 'Now,' says the Bible, 'until you realize that you are up against a power like that, you have not started to think clearly. If you do not realize that, all the while you are in this life and in this world, there will be this terrible infernal power within you and around and about you, then you are a mere novice in these matters! The fact is that here in this world there are principalities and powers, rulers of the darkness of this world, spiritual wickedness in the heavenly places, begging, beseeching you, getting you down.' That is the biblical doctrine of sin. That is the terrible thing which is revealed to us in this psalm. The first step is that man must realize and confess his sinfulness.

Actually this fifty-first psalm is what you

might call, if you like, 'A prayer of a backslider'. It was the prayer of a man who had believed God and had experienced the gracious dealings of God. It is about a man who falls though he knows the truth. But that does not make any difference. What David tells us here about sin is always true of sin, whether it is the sin of a believer or an unbeliever. Sin never changes its character, and therefore what David has to say about sin is something that is always a universal truth about sin. Here, then, we are shown the steps and the stages through which a man inevitably passes when he becomes convinced and convicted of his sin. I merely want to pick them out and underline them.

The first is this. *He comes to a knowledge of and an acknowledgment of the fact that he has sinned.* Listen to David in verse 3: 'For I acknowledge my transgressions: and my sin is ever before me.' The first thing, therefore, that happens to a man when he becomes convinced and convicted of sin is that he faces his sin and really looks at what he has done in an honest manner. This whole story tells us that that was exactly what David had not done. Now is there not something almost incredible about this, that a man could do the things which David did and yet really not face them? Surely David must have felt he was doing wrong; yet he did it! He never really faced the fact of wrongdoing, and he went on refusing to face it. And, having done these terrible things, David would still not have faced them, were it not that God sent the prophet Nathan to him and made him face them by giving him details of the same thing as it happened in a different form. Thus David saw, and he was humbled to the dust. That is how he came to write this fifty-first psalm. This is always the first step. We must stop and think, we must pause for a moment and face ourselves, and face the life we have lived and what we have done and what we are doing.

Now I know that this is very unpleasant, and people dislike a gospel that says a thing like that. But if you want to know God's salvation you have to repent, and the first step is conviction of sin, and the first way to become convicted of sin is to stop and look at yourself. Is it not amazing, I ask again, that David could do the things he did and not face them? There are all the things he has done, but he carries on. How can he do so? There is only one way of carrying on in such a position and that is to refuse to face what you are doing and to stop to think. That is why I do not denounce the so-called pleasure mania, which is just an attempt on the part of people to run away from this. It is unpleasant to have to spend a night with yourself and ask, 'What kind of life am I living? What are the things I fondle in my imagination and in my mind?' Yet this is absolutely essential; we have to stop and face ourselves and the life we are living. We are all remarkably like David. How easy it is to excuse things in ourselves, to pass them by and to dismiss them! Yet we are so ready to denounce with fury the same things when we see them in another, or when a like case is put before us. This is part of human nature. This is true of all of us as the result of the Fall and of sin. We devise all these methods of running away from ourselves. Let me ask a simple question at this point: 'Have you faced yourself?' Forget everybody else. Hold up a mirror before yourself, look back across your life, look at the things you have thought and done and said, look at the kind of life you are living. Are you satisfied with it? Do you pass in other people's lives some of the things which you yourself do? Would you pass them as having a clean sheet? The first call to man by God is to be honest, to stop arguing and to face himself. Let him examine himself. And, yes, let me go still further, let us stop arguing about religion and theology and let us for once just look at ourselves honestly and squarely. That is the first step. 'I acknowledge my transgressions: and my sin is ever before me.' Have you faced it, have you really examined yourself and really looked into your own heart? There is no hope for a man who does not do that, and the truth about the modern world is that people are running away from just this. They are crowding into cinemas, reading novels—anything to fill up their lives and keep them from thinking.

I say that you have to fight for your life and you have to fight for your soul. The world will do everything to prevent you facing yourself. My dear friend, let me appeal to you. Look at yourself. Forget everybody and everything else. It is the first step in the knowledge of God and in the experience of His glorious salvation.

But let me hurry on to the second step. The second step is *a recognition of the exact character or nature of what we have done.* That is put here very perfectly in three words. The first is the word 'transgressions', the second is 'iniquity', and 'sin' is the third. Now let me say a little about these three words.

What does *'transgression'* mean? It means rebellion, it means the uprising of the will against authority, and especially against a person of authority. That is the meaning of transgression. 'Blot out my transgressions.' In other words, David admits he has transgressed, he admits he has rebelled. He has rebelled against an authority, against someone. His own will has risen up within him and he has asserted himself. He has been governed by desire and has allowed himself to be swayed by lust. Transgression means a desire to have our own way, a desire to do what we want to do, what we like doing. It involves a deliberate choice, it involves an act of active defiance. It always means that we do something that our own

conscience tells us to be wrong. It is a wilful, deliberate act of disobedience, a violation of authority—
that is the meaning of transgression. Every man
who repents realizes that he is guilty of that. He is
prepared to admit, 'Yes, I did it, though I knew it
was wrong! I knew the voice within me, my conscience, said no, but I did it. I was a rebel, I did it
deliberately!'

'Iniquity', what does that mean? Well, iniquity
means that an act is twisted or that it is bent. It
means perversion, and this is obvious in the case of
David. 'Wash me throughly from mine iniquity!—
the foul thing, that dastardly thing. What was it in
me that made me do it? That twist, the perversion!
How perverted I must have been to do that!' You
remember what David had done. I need not stay to
emphasize the twist, and his bent condition, and
the perversion of it all. And, in this respect, how
true this is of every act of which we are all guilty.
You and I may not be guilty of murder, thank God!
We are not guilty of some of the other things of
which David was guilty. But I ask you as you examine yourself, do you not see that so many things you
do are twisted and perverted? Do you not see that
so many of your actions in life are bent? Jealousy
and envy and malice—how horrible the twist! The
desire that evil may come to someone, the dislike of
praise of another—evil thoughts, bent, twisted,
ugly, foul—'iniquity'! And we are all guilty of iniq-

uity. Is there anyone who would like to deny that there is such a twist in him, and that so many of his actions have had this horrible twist and perversion in them?

And, then, concerning the last word, 'sin'. What does sin mean? Sin means missing the mark, and that is a very good way of putting it. The thought it conveys is this—that we are not living as we ought to be living. There is a man aiming at a mark; there is his target. He shoots, but he misses it. He has missed the mark. It means that we are not what we should be, that we are 'off the straight'. That is what sin always means. It indicates that a man is living a life which he was not meant to live. It shows that he is not treading the path God has marked out for him. He does not go straight ahead. He does not keep an even keel. There is a backward and a forward movement, there is a lack of straightness in it.

I need not press these points. I know that every person in this congregation must recognize that he or she is guilty of these three things—transgression (or rebellion), iniquity (or perversion, twist, bent actions) and sin (i.e., missing the mark, not getting there, not being what we ought to be, what we are meant to be, going here, there and everywhere instead of where we ought to be going—straight forward). The second step in the conviction of sin and the confession of sin is that man recognizes that that is the character of his life and actions.

Then step number three is that *man realizes and confesses that all this is done against God and before God.* 'Against thee, thee only, have I sinned, and done this evil in thy sight.' 'Surely', says someone, 'that must be wrong? David ought to have said, "Against Bathsheba, against Uriah, against the men who were killed in that battle, against Israel and my people have I sinned." But he says, "Against thee, thee only . . . "' Ah, he is quite right! He does not deny that he has sinned against the others, but here he is going a step further forward. He realizes that his actions are not simply actions in and of themselves. He sees that they not only affect and involve other people, but the real essence is that he has sinned against God. Now that is the essential difference between *remorse* and *repentance.* A man who suffers remorse is one who realizes he has done wrong, but he has not *repented* until he realizes that he has sinned against God.

Why should he feel that? Let me try to answer the question in the following manner. Sin, you see, means a violation of what God has made, and of what God intended man to be. Let me put it, in a preliminary fashion, in this form. When a man sins, he is not only doing certain things himself which he should not do; he is sinning against human nature, he is letting it down. He is sinning, therefore, against humanity, and because of that he is sinning against God who made man. God made man perfect, and God intended man to live that perfect life. He gave him the possibility of doing so, and when a man sins he lets God down. 'Against *thee, thee only*, have I sinned.' I have violated what God intended man to be. I am twisting and perverting God's creation. Every time I sin I am violating God's holy law. The Ten Commandments, the moral law, the common idea of decency in human nature—all this is derived from God. It is there, we are all aware of it, and every time I am guilty of transgression or iniquity or sin, I am violating the holy law of God, and the plan laid down for man's life. Indeed, I am also violating, as I have reminded you, my conscience within me. Conscience has been placed in me by God. I am not responsible for it. How often have we wished that we did not have a conscience! But it is there. You know that inward voice that speaks and tells you not to do a thing. If you do it you are violating the rule of God. It is also sin against God because it means that we do all these things in spite of His goodness to us. I think that was the thing that broke the heart of David more than anything else. God had been so good to him. He was only a shepherd boy and God had made him king of this great kingdom and granted him such abundant blessings. Yet David confesses,

'I have done this dastardly thing.' He says, 'Against thee, thee only, have I sinned.'

God gave you the gift of life. You did not bring yourself into this world, and you are a unique personality. He has showered His blessings upon you. He has put you in a family, surrounded you by love. He has sent you food and shelter. He could have withheld all that. Think of the goodness God has bestowed upon you in different ways! Yet we defy Him! We sin against Him and against His amazing goodness and kindness and love with respect to us!

What is the next step? The next step is that *man finds that he has absolutely no excuse or plea.* 'Against thee, thee only, have I sinned, and done this evil in thy sight: that thou mightest be justified when thou speakest, and be clear when thou judgest.' In other words, David is telling God: 'I haven't a single excuse. I have no plea. There is nothing to be said for me. There is no reason for what I have done. The whole thing was the result of utter wilfulness. I am altogether wrong. I have nothing to plead in mitigation.' I want to emphasize this. I say that this is an absolutely essential part of repentance and of conviction of sin. I therefore plead with you to examine yourselves and examine your actions. Can you justify all you have done? Can you really put up a plea of mitigation? Let me take up the position of Nathan the prophet. What if I stood in this pulpit and described your life to you in a parable about somebody else? Would you see this? We must examine ourselves in this respect. Let me put it bluntly, by putting it to you like this. As long as you are in the position of trying to justify yourself you have not repented. As long as you are clinging on to any attempt at self-justification and self-righteousness, I say you have not repented. Surely the man who is repentant is the man who, like David, says: 'There is not a single excuse. I see it clearly. I have no justification. The things which I see in my life—I hate them, I had no business to do them, I did them wilfully, I knew it was wrong. I admit it! I frankly confess it— "that thou mightest be justified when thou speakest, and be clear when thou judgest".' Do you feel that God is rather hard on you when He condemns you? Do you feel that God would be dealing unfairly with you if you ever found yourself in hell? If you do, you have not repented. I would emphasize that the test of repentance is this, that a man having looked at himself, and at his own heart and life, says to himself: 'I deserve nothing but hell, and if God sends me there, I haven't a single complaint to make. I deserve nothing better!' That is an essential part of repentance, and without repentance there is no salvation. The man, I say, who has a conviction of sin is the man who comes to these steps. And that brings me to the last.

The last step is that *he realizes and recognizes*

that his very nature is essentially evil. 'Behold, I was shapen in iniquity; and in sin did my mother conceive me.' You see the steps? The first thing is that he stops and faces the facts, he looks at himself. Then, in the second step, he recognizes the actions of which he has been guilty and admits they are wrong in three respects. And then he says, 'Yes, but this involves God, and I have sinned against God.' The next step comes when he acknowledges, 'I am without a single plea and excuse.' But then he asks himself: 'What made me do it? Whatever brought me to that? What is it about me that makes me capable of all these things—jealousy, envy, hatred, malice, avarice, desire, lust, passion?' Then at last he comes to see it, and declares: 'My very nature must be corrupt, my very heart must be evil! It is not the world outside me, it is something *in* me that is rotten!' In other words, the ultimate step in this conviction of sin is that man rises from a realization of his sins to a realization of *sin* and of his utter worthlessness.

This last step is the one which Paul describes in the seventh chapter of the Epistle to the Romans: 'I know that in me (that is, in my flesh,) dwelleth no good thing . . . O wretched man that I am! who shall deliver me from the body of this death?' (verses 18,24). That is, he declares: 'Within me I am rotten, I am foul, my heart is black. It is not merely that I do the things which I should not do, it is *I myself*. It is that I have a desire to do these things, I want to do them. Why? Because there is that in me which responds to the attraction of evil. It is that which bothers me. It is that I am capable of it and that I enjoy it. It is my heart, it is not the world.' As Shakespeare put it,

> *The fault, dear Brutus, is not in our stars,*
> *But in ourselves, that we are underlings.*

'Behold, I was shapen in iniquity; and in sin did my mother conceive me.' From the moment of my birth into this world there is a tendency in me towards evil; there is something twisted and perverted. It is in me; it is part of my being and nature.

Those, then, are the steps in conviction of sin and in confession of sin.

If you see the truth of what I have been trying to say, do you not feel like crying out with David, 'Have mercy upon me, O God'? That is the right thing, the only thing to do, my friend. If you see yourself as one who has sinned, then, I beseech you, fly to God, cast yourself upon His mercy. You will not do it in vain. You will find He has made full provision for you. He sent the Son of His love into this world just for you, to die for your sin on Calvary's hill. Your sin has been punished, He has blotted it out there, He will wash you and make you whiter than snow, He will give you everything you need. Hasten to Him. If you have seen the need, you will do so. The man who sees it, as David saw it, immediately cries out, 'Have mercy upon me, O God . . . wash me'. Do the same and your prayer will be gloriously answered, and you will know the joy of God's great salvation.

Psalm 51:1-2

'Have mercy upon me,
O God, according to thy lovingkindness:
according unto the multitude of thy
tender mercies blot out my transgressions.
Wash me throughly from mine iniquity,
and cleanse me from my sin'.

II

THE SINNER'S HELPLESSNESS

◆

Psalm 51:1-2

We shall not confine ourselves exclusively to these two verses because, as you will observe, the sentiments are repeated again: 'Purge me with hyssop, and I shall be clean: wash me, and I shall be whiter than snow . . . Hide thy face from my sins, and blot out all mine iniquities' (verses 7 and 9).

As we continue with our study of this psalm, let me remind you that my main reason for doing so is that it contains within itself the main steps and stages in connection with the whole question of salvation and our relationship to God. That is the most important and vital question in this world—our relationship to God. It is the most important

◆

question because obviously it is a question that is inevitable. There are many things in this life which are uncertain; but one thing is absolutely certain, and that is that we have to go out of it. And then what happens? 'Well, I do not believe there is anything beyond death,' says someone. But can you prove it, are you prepared to risk it? Can you not see that you hold your belief without any proof or evidence? The certain fact is that we are going out of this world. We all of us must needs die, and then—'ay, there's the rub', as Shakespeare put it:

> . . . the dread of something after death,—
> The undiscover'd country, from whose bourn
> No traveller returns—

that is the thing that makes 'cowards of us all'. And that is why the most important thing in life is for us to know how to meet God. Fortunately this psalm deals with that in a perfect manner. It tells us that there are very definite steps and stages, there are certain things which are always present in this matter of salvation and coming to God.

Let me remind you once more that this fifty-first psalm, written by David, king of Israel, is really the psalm of a backslider, the psalm of a man who knew he had committed a terrible crime. He was guilty of adultery and murder and deceit and many other things, and though he had done these things he was perfectly happy for a while, and seemed to be enjoying the fruit of all his evil, vicious, vile deeds. But God sent Nathan the prophet to him, and Nathan propounded a parable in which he was really telling David what he had done. And David suddenly saw the truth and saw the sin of which he was guilty. The result was that he wrote this fifty-first psalm. I say it is essentially the psalm of a backslider; but what David has to show us here about sin is always true, whether it is in a sinner or a backslider, whether it is in a man who has believed in Christ or not. Sin has always the same terrible characteristics. So that in this psalm we really get one of the most perfect and classic accounts of sin and how a man can get rid of his sin. It is generally called the great psalm of repentance. So it is; it tells us everything that is essential concerning repentance.

Now I remind you of all that because I am anxious to impress the point that there is most definitely a common pattern in this experience of salvation. I put it in that form in order to help certain people who may be unhappy about this whole question of salvation. There are such people; they are fully aware that there is something wrong in their lives, they meet other people who were once as they are, but who seem to have found wonderful joy and release, and who talk about salvation. These troubled people say, 'I want to know something about that. I wish I had it, I wish I had the experience of these other people. How is one to obtain it?' Now my reply is that there are certain things that are always present in the typical, characteristic, Christian experience, and you will find them described everywhere. Take, for instance, the Bible itself: there is a common pattern to all the cases that are described in the Bible, there are certain things that are present in all, and those are the things in which we are interested. Or if you take up the biographies of Christian people or read the lives of saints, you cannot do so without discovering this common pattern. Certain things are always present, and that is why, if we are not aware of these things in ourselves, we are just not Christian. Or take your hymn-book: different men wrote the hymns, but they all say the same thing. There is this common element, this common pattern. The Christian experience is something quite definite, it is quite concrete; that is why a man can really test himself and discover whether he is Christian or not. The New Testament exhorts him to do so, and it is asking of him something that can be done. There is no need for uncertainty in your mind; it can be discovered quite easily. Let us never think of the Christian position as some vague, indefinite, nebulous thing somewhere up in the air. No, the Christian position is a very definite one; it is one of the most concrete things in life. Therefore we can apply tests.

Very well, there is a common pattern; and of course that is not surprising, for this work is the work of the Holy Spirit. No man can become a Christian without the work of the Holy Spirit in his soul, and it is not surprising that He tends to do the same things in all cases. He leaves certain marks, and they are very definite. Yet, having said that, at the same time we must be careful lest we standardize the Christian experience in a wrong way and insist upon certain particular details in every case. I say this by way of warning, because I have found people in trouble about this whole matter because somebody has attempted to standardize the Christian experience in detail, as well as in big principles.

Let me give you one illustration of what I mean. Anybody who has ever read John Bunyan's *Grace Abounding* will know that in that book John Bunyan tells us that he passed through an agony of repentance that lasted for eighteen long months, and during those eighteen months he lived a life which was nothing but sheer agony. There were times when he felt so miserable and so unhappy that, on one occasion, seeing some geese in a field, he wished he were something like those geese so that he need not experience this agony of repentance. Another day he tells us that he saw himself, as it were, swayed over the open jaws of hell and he could smell brimstone in the air. Now I have met

people who have said something like this to me:
'You know, my greatest desire in life is to be a
Christian; I have been trying for years.' When I ask,
'What is the hindrance?', they say, 'I have never
repented.' 'On what grounds do you tell me that?' I
ask. They say, 'I have never felt like John Bunyan
and wished I had been a beast that lacked the
quality of human nature; I have never felt or seen
myself suspended over the open jaws of hell; I have
never smelt the brimstone in the air.' And because
they have not had these particular experiences that
John Bunyan had, they feel they have not
repented. I once knew a man who was a Christian
himself and who expressed great concern about the
state of his son. He was quite satisfied in his own
mind that his son was not a Christian, and when I
asked him why, he said that his son had never had
'the Damascus road experience'. He had had something like that himself, his conversion had come
rather suddenly; and because his son had not had
some sudden experience, he said his son was not
converted. That is what I mean when I say that we
must be careful not to standardize this common
experience in the matter of particular details.
There are many saints in heaven today who have
never had the particular feelings that John Bunyan
had, but they repented as certainly as John
Bunyan repented.

Well, let us be very careful about that. Or let

me put it like this: we must be very careful that we do not insist upon the various steps and stages described in this psalm happening in a particular chronological order. There are some people who are always anxious to standardize everything and I am not here to contend for that. What I am saying is that in every case of conversion, in every case of repentance, there are certain common elements. There is a common pattern, but in some cases one thing comes first and the other follows, in other cases the second thing comes first and the first follows. I do not say it must happen in a standard manner, but I do say that in the absence of certain things we have never repented, and without repentance we are not Christian.

Another way in which we can look at it is this. There are certain people who seem to avoid this whole question for this reason. They say, 'You know, that fifty-first psalm is, as you say very rightly, a great psalm on the question of repentance. It is not surprising that David felt as he did in view of the things he had been doing. But, you know, I really do not feel very interested in your fifty-first psalm because, thank God, I have never committed adultery, I have never committed murder. It is all right for a man who has done that kind of thing, but do you expect me to experience the same things that David experienced? If I had been guilty of great sin I should feel like that. But do you expect me to feel as David felt?' There are many in such a position, and the simple answer to such people is that repentance is in no sense dependent upon the type or the kind of sin which you have committed.

This is what David says about himself as a sinner, but let me remind you of another type of man. Take a man whose hymns we delight to sing, Charles Wesley. Now Charles Wesley never committed adultery or murder, he was never guilty of the things of which David was guilty at this point in his life. Charles Wesley was a very good man; he was the son of a clergyman, and a particularly devout clergyman, and he had an exceptional mother, a particularly holy woman. Here he is, brought up in a rectory, and when he goes to Oxford with his brother John they form the Holy Club that they might live good lives. Even as undergraduates in Oxford they went to preach in prisons, they gave their money to help poor people. He always lived a good life and did everything to be godly and devout and to please God. Yet you remember what he says of himself—things which are quite as drastic as what David tells us:

> *Just and holy is Thy Name,*
> *I am all unrighteousness;*
> *Vile and full of sin I am,*

says this excellent young man, though he is not guilty of David's sins. And I could multiply examples. Take, for instance, that great hymn of Augustus Toplady. Here is another man who had never been guilty of the things of which David was guilty; he was always a good man. But you remember what he says about himself:

Foul, I to the fountain fly;
Wash me, Saviour, or I die.

O my dear friend, you cannot avoid the issue like that. The facts are against you. The feeling of repentance is not dependent upon the particular nature of the sin committed. The Bible proves that, the hymns prove that, the Christian biographies prove the same thing.

Then there are others who seem to be in difficulty on this point. They say that surely this is all a question of personality, a man's particular type or kind of personality. They say that they have been reading a bit of psychology, and have discovered that psychologists say there is a sort of 'twice-born' type of individual. This twice-born type of individual, according to the psychologist, is the man who spends a good deal of his time examining himself. Then there is another type of man who is called the 'once-born' type of man. He does not spend his time examining his own soul. This man is a cultured, more balanced type, not introspective and given to morbidity like the twice-born type. Now they say that they are prepared to grant us that certain people of the twice-born type, such as David, Saul of Tarsus, John and Charles Wesley, Augustus Toplady, are likely to have and seem to need a great experience of repentance; but in the case of the once-born type there is no need to feel such an agony of repentance, as they are all right as they are. As all people are different, why should we all have to experience the same thing? On the surface that is a very plausible statement and argument. But again we have nothing to do but to bring this argument to the light of facts. What are the facts? The facts are these. You go through your Bible and look at these heroes of the faith in the Old and the New Testament, and nothing will strike you more than this, the amazing and obvious natural differences between the different people mentioned. I do not hesitate to assert that in the Bible you have all the psychological combinations of temperament and character and make-up and anything else you may like to add. Look at the twelve disciples. John and Peter were quite different men. Paul is different again. These are sheer facts. The Bible itself answers this theory, and as you read the history of the church through the ages you will find exactly the same thing. You will find within the Christian church the mercurial and excitable type and the phlegmatic type, the sensitive and the almost callous type; and yet they will all say the same things about this matter. I assert that every conceivable type is represented in the Christian church today; and yet, if we could pick them out and get their testimony, they would all make this statement about seeing themselves as sinners and flying to the fountain for cleansing. No, it has nothing to do with temperament, nothing whatsoever. The facts again are sufficient to disprove the contention. I trust, therefore, that there is no one in confusion any longer on that particular score.

My contention is that there are certain things that are always present in every case of conversion and of salvation, and I suggest that if you do not find these things somewhere in your life or experience, you are not entitled to use the name Christian with regard to yourself. We have already looked at certain things. These are the first things, that the man who repents is a man who faces himself and looks at himself. No man has ever become a Christian without stopping to look at himself. The world does its best to prevent a man looking at himself; it keeps him rushing here and there—anything to stop his looking at himself. But a Christian is a man who has seen himself and seen what he has done. He has seen his transgressions, his iniquity, his sin. He realizes the meaning of his actions. He realizes he has sinned against God; and he has seen that his actual nature is itself sinful. I would call that 'the sinner awakening', facing himself and realizing the initial truths about himself. But we do not stop at that; we must go on.

The next point is this. No man has ever repented and become a Christian without *an element of concern and feeling entering into his consciousness with regard to his state and condition.* That is obvious in this psalm: 'Have mercy upon me, O God.' The man who wrote this psalm was feeling desperate. He felt a great concern about his state and condition. He cannot get away from it, it is the most important problem in his life and existence. David was a king, and a very wealthy king, and he had a very wealthy kingdom; but when he realized this truth about himself, all his wealth and power and position could not satisfy him. This was the thing that mattered, and he said, 'I must find peace about this; I must get right with God.' It had become the biggest thing in his life. I need not stay with this; surely it is more or less obvious. I ask you again to read your Bible, to read the biographies of the saints, to read your hymn-book, and you will find that every man who has ever repented has passed through that particular phase and experience. He has felt a concern about his soul and about his relationship to God. I have nothing to add at this point, but just to ask a simple question. Have you ever been concerned about yourself and the state of your soul? Have you any anxiety about it, have you ever known restlessness about it, has the

question of your soul worried or troubled you? I say
again that if it has not, church membership is of no
use to you, and your use of the Christian designation is utterly misleading. This is something
inevitable and unavoidable in the case of all who
repent and become Christian.

Let me go further and put it in this form. I
imagine someone saying to me, 'I have never felt
that great concern. I do not see that I need to feel
that concern. I have been brought up in a religious
manner, I have gone to places of worship, I have
tried to do good, I have tried to give the helping
hand. Surely I am not expected to know this great
concern of which you are speaking.' Well, my reply
is that I am not at all sure but that to feel like that
is just the greatest sin of all. Let me put it in this
way. I ask you again to look at the saints. If these
godly people, these saintly men and women to
whom I have referred, have seen themselves as sinners in the sight of God, why are you different? I
just challenge you on this point. I say there has
never been a saint on the face of this earth who has
not seen himself as a vile sinner; so that if you do
not feel that you are a vile sinner you are unlike the
saints. But wait a minute, let me come a little bit
nearer. I would invite you to try to consider for a
moment who God is and what God is. I remember
reading an article by a man who criticized that
hymn of Charles Wesley's, where Charles Wesley

◆

said, 'I am all unrighteousness' and 'Vile and full of sin I am'. The man criticized it in this way: he said, 'Fancy a man seeking employment approaching the man who is going to employ him and in the interview saying to him, "Vile and full of sin I am." He would not get the job.' And he thought that that disposed of the whole matter. But you see what he had forgotten. I do not myself see any reason why a man should speak like that to a fellow human being who he knows is the same as himself, but Charles Wesley was not speaking of himself in the presence of man, he was addressing God. And 'God is light, and in him is no darkness at all' (1 John 1:5). Can you conceive of that? God is utter, absolute holiness; there is no spot, there is no blemish. Try to conceive of that. He is the one we are concerned about—God. And what does God demand of us? Well, I will tell you: 'Thou shalt love the Lord thy God with all thy heart, and with all thy soul, and with all thy strength, and with all thy mind; and thy neighbour as thyself' (Luke 10:27). My friend, the question is not whether you have committed adultery or murder. It is this: have you loved and are you loving God with all your heart and all your soul and all your mind and all your strength? If you are not, you are a sinner. God demands that of you, and He has a right to demand it of us, for He is God, and He has made us, and He has made us for Himself. 'The chief end of man is

to glorify God', and not to glorify God is the greatest sin of all. Do we glorify God? Do we thank Him
day by day for His goodness, mercy and gracious-
ness to us? Do we ascribe praise and honour and
glory to Him? Is it our chief concern that He may
be glorified more and more? Jesus Christ said that
His greatest object in life was that the Father
might be glorified. Every man is called upon to do
the same thing, and not to do that is to be sinful.
You remember how Daniel put all this to another
king—Belshazzar. He says, 'The God in whose
hand thy breath is, and whose are all thy ways,
hast thou not glorified' (Daniel 5:23). The essence of
sin is not so much to be guilty of particular actions;
it is not to be glorifying God, it is not to be living our
life for God. God put man on the earth that he
might do that, and a refusal or failure to do that is
the very essence of sin. That is why every man who
repents always feels this concern about his soul
and has a feeling of desperation about himself. Do
you serve God, do you love God, do you seek God,
do you try to glorify God? That is the first thing.

The second thing I want to mention is *the
desire for pardon*. 'Have mercy upon me, O God,
according to thy lovingkindness: according unto
the multitude of thy tender mercies blot out my
transgressions. Wash me throughly from mine iniquity, and cleanse me from my sin.' In other words,
a man who repents is always a man who is aware

of his guilt. He says, 'When I face and think of God, and when I face God's law and God's standard, I am aware of the fact that I am guilty. I have not lived that sort of life; there have been days when I have not prayed to God, I have not thanked Him, and I have forgotten Him altogether. Immediately I begin to examine myself I find I have done things which I knew were wrong; I have been guilty of sin in the mind and thought and imagination. I know it.' He is aware of his guilt, and being aware of this he has a desire to be pardoned. He knows what David meant when he said, 'Blot out my transgressions.' He desires to be cleansed, he has a feeling that he is unclean. He knows that he has become bespattered and besmirched by evil and sin and that which is wrong. He knows that he is not clean within as well as without; he has become stained. Therefore he knows this desire to be washed, to be cleansed, yes, to be purged from his iniquity.

The next thing that is characteristic of every truly repentant soul, and in every person who is truly Christian, is *an awareness, a consciousness of utter helplessness*. You see it coming out in David's psalm. He does not know what to do with himself. What is the matter with him? He cannot quieten his own conscience. His conscience was accusing him, and whatever he did he could not silence it; it was always holding his sin before him. Conscience when it awakes is a terrible thing, and sooner or later every man's conscience must awaken. Some men go through a long life and it does not seem to awaken; but they have not finished. They have to come to a death-bed, and sometimes it only awakens there, and sometimes beyond even that. Do you remember when the rich man who died saw the beggar in Abraham's bosom (Luke 16:19-31), his conscience awoke there in hell? Conscience is a terrible thing. David is here trying to quieten his conscience, but he cannot do it. He would give everything to quieten his conscience—he is a wealthy man, he has flocks and herds—but he cannot do it. When you look back across your life and see certain things, would you not like to get rid of them, to erase and blot them out, to remove the stain? But it cannot be done. David realized that, and every man who has become a Christian realizes it. He likewise cannot find peace; he is doing everything he can, but he cannot find peace. He cannot sleep; this thing is there, it is always before him, he cannot get away from it. I do not say that of necessity you need have a particular feeling, but I do say that no man is a Christian unless at some time he has known that terrible searching for peace, for rest and for quiet. The great St Augustine knew it; for quite a period he had this restlessness of soul and at last he cried out, 'Thou hast made us for Thyself, and our souls are restless until they find their rest in Thee.' Have you known this restlessness, have you known this search for peace and quiet of conscience and of mind and of heart in an attempt to get rid of the sense of guilt?

David was aware of his utter helplessness. Indeed he goes further, he knows he cannot do anything about it. Listen to him: 'For thou desirest not sacrifice; else would I give it: thou delightest not in burnt offering.' Poor David, how well I understand him! As I have reminded you, he was a wealthy man, and he says that if it were a question of offering sacrifices he would do it. 'I have flocks and herds; I could make a great offering. But "the cattle on a thousand hills" are Thine, the whole created universe is Thine; I can give Thee nothing. If it were sufficient I would do it, but Thou desirest not sacrifice.' Every man who truly repents knows exactly what that means. You see, you start thinking when the conscience awakes, and you say, 'I am going to live a better life, I am going to give up certain things and do other things.' And on and on you go, but still you cannot find peace and rest and quiet; and on you go again until at last you see it will never be enough, and you realize your complete, entire, absolute helplessness. O my friend, have you still any vestige of self-confidence left? Do you still feel you can make yourself a Christian? Do you feel the life you are living is going to satisfy God? I ask again, do you love the Lord your God with all your heart, with all your soul, with all your mind, and with all your strength, and your neighbour as yourself? That is God's law, those are the first and the second great commandments. You will be judged by that. Cease to trust to your own self-righteousness, and to this 'twenty shillings in the pound' morality and doing good. Face God and realize you can do nothing. You are utterly helpless. 'Thou desirest not sacrifice; else would I give it.'

But, lastly, the most amazing thing of all to the man who repents and becomes a Christian is his *new attitude towards God*. It is so obvious here in the case of David. What a remarkable thing it is! I do not hesitate to assert that this is perhaps the most subtle and delicate test of all as to whether we have repented, or where we are: our attitude towards God. Have you noticed it in the psalm? The one against whom David has sinned is God, and yet the one he desires above all is God. That is the difference between remorse and repentance. The man who has not repented, but who is only experiencing remorse, when he realizes he has done something against God, avoids God. You remember Adam and Eve at the beginning; they committed sin and they tried to hide themselves from God. They were not repentant at that point. The man who has not been dealt with by the Spirit of God and has not been convinced and convicted, tries to get away from God, to avoid Him at all costs. He does not think, he does not read the Bible, he does not pray; he does

◆

everything he can not to think about these things. But the extraordinary thing about the man who is convicted of sin by the Holy Spirit is that though he knows he has sinned against God, it is God he wants—'Be merciful to me, O God.' He wants to be with God—that is the peculiar paradox of repentance, wanting the one I have offended! I put it therefore in this form. The impenitent avoids God: the penitent knows that no one but God can really satisfy. And following that, I say this about him, that though he knows that he has no claim upon God, he nevertheless turns to God and begins to speak to Him. He believes that God can help him, and he knows that no one else can—burnt offering, sacrifices, all are insufficient. All the cleansing of the world is not enough. 'What can I do?' he says; 'How can I get rid of the stain?' There is only one who can do it and that is God Himself.

But the most wonderful thing of all—and I leave it to the end—is this: the repentant sinner not only knows that God has the power to remove the stain and the guilt of his sin; he knows, wonder of wonders, that God is ready to do it and willing to do it. Listen to David—'Be merciful to me, O God.' He knows God is merciful. What else? 'Have mercy upon me, according to thy lovingkindness'—what glorious words! But he does not stop even at that; he adds this—'according unto the multitude of thy tender mercies blot out my transgressions'. That is the explanation of the paradox of the penitent: he knows he has sinned against this holy God, and yet he knows that with God there is loving-kindness, with God there is a multitude of tender mercies, and he casts himself upon this mercy—'Have mercy upon me, O God.' You remember how Christ put it in His parable of that poor publican who went up to the temple to pray; he was so conscious of his sin he could not lift up his eyes to heaven, but cried out, saying, 'God be merciful to me a sinner' (Luke 18:13).

How did David know all this about God? The answer is, of course, that he had experienced it. God had blessed him; God had been good to him; God had been kind to him; and here he is in his terrible sin against God. David says, 'I can venture to go to Him. I have been a liar, I have been a murderer, I have been the cause of the death of innocent people. No man will forgive me, but though God is absolutely holy I know that He has mercy. He has loving-kindness, He has a multitude of tender mercies. I can venture to go to Him, and He will not reject me.'

David knew that, but, my friend, you and I know something infinitely more. Is there anyone who is conscious of sin and guilt, but who has not found peace? Are you searching for it? I ask you, have you turned to God? 'But if only you knew what I had done, you would not tell me to turn to God,' says someone; 'I am afraid of God.' My friend, let me beseech you to turn to God just as you are. David knew He was merciful; he knew He had loving-kindness and a multitude of tender mercies; but you and I are privileged to know that in an infinitely greater and bigger way. What do the bread and wine on the communion table mean? They are a reminder, a memorial of the fact that once upon a time, nearly two thousand years ago, this God of mercy, this God of loving-kindness, this God of the multitude of tender mercies, sent His only begotten Son into this world. And He sent Him with one object, and that was that He might bear the guilt of your sin and mine. He laid our sins upon Him and He punished them there. God has punished your sins in Christ, and there offers His free pardon and forgiveness.

> *Venture on Him, venture wholly,*
> *Let no other trust intrude.*

This, I say, is the most amazing thing in the world, that the God we have offended is the God who has provided the way of salvation. It is this amazing love of God, again, that baffles one because of its immensity. 'God so loved the world, that he gave his only begotten Son, that whosoever believeth in him should not perish, but have everlasting life' (John 3:16). That is the answer. It is also the measure of sin. You see, God had to do that, God had to deal with sin. Sin is as terrible as that.

◆

Your good works are not enough to atone for it, otherwise Christ would never have died. Why did Christ go to the cross, why did Christ die?

> *There is only one answer:*
> *There was no other good enough*
> *To pay the price of sin;*
> *He only could unlock the gate*
> *Of heaven and let us in.*

But, thank God, He has done it, and therefore:

> *Just as I am, without one plea,*
> *But that Thy blood was shed for me,*
> *And that Thou biddst me come to Thee,*
> *O Lamb of God, I come.*

Are you concerned about your soul? Do you realize the position you are in? Is this troubling you, are you facing it? I ask, is it not time you did? There is God—unavoidable. You have to face Him, and the only way to do so is in Jesus Christ. Believe on Him, give yourself to Him, and be eternally saved.

◆

Psalm 51:10a

'Create in me a clean heart, O God'.

III

THE SINNER'S CENTRAL NEED

◆

Psalm 51:10a

I would remind you again that I am calling attention to this psalm not only because it is the great classic statement on the whole doctrine of repentance, but because at the same time it reminds us in a very clear and forcible manner of some of the steps and stages through which anyone must of necessity pass who is to become truly Christian. There are certain things which are essential to the Christian position. I make no apology for making such a statement. I think one of the greatest tragedies of the hour is that an idea of vagueness should have entered into the average person's conception as to what constitutes a Christian. There is

◆

no difficulty in the New Testament in discovering what made one a Christian. Certain people were called Christians for a very specific reason, and it was such a definite thing that it was dangerous to be a Christian at times. There is no doubt or vagueness in the New Testament, and there have been other times in the history of the church when the position of the Christian has been perfectly clear and perfectly definite. I say it is one of the major tragedies of this twentieth century that a loose conception as to what constitutes Christianity, and what makes a man a Christian, has crept in. We need not be concerned about the causes of that at this point. We know that ultimately it is to be traced back to a denial of the unique authority of this Book, and to the substitution of human ideas for divine revelation.

Here in this psalm, in a very definite form, are gathered together for us some of these essential things which are always part and parcel of the true Christian experience. I say again that unless we are aware of these things in ourselves in a certain measure or to a certain extent, we are in no sense entitled to apply the designation Christian to ourselves. Here we have at one and the same time a somewhat terrifying exposure of the need of mankind in sin, and the provision that is made for us in the gospel of our Lord and Saviour Jesus Christ. You do not get that in its fulness in this

psalm, but you get an introduction in a most extraordinary manner. Here is expressed in embryo
what we have in greater fulness in the New
Testament. We are looking at it in this way because
the nature of man apart from Christ is expressed
here in such a clear and striking manner.

Let me summarize the point at which we have
arrived in our previous studies of this psalm. There
are certain steps before one ever becomes a
Christian, and the first is that a man has got to stop
and think. I say it is impossible to be a Christian
without thinking. Now I know there are many people who think a man is Christian because he does
not think and that those who are outside Christ
have a monopoly of thought. Yet the whole case of
the Bible is that a man does not even begin to
become a Christian until he thinks. What does he
think about? He thinks about himself. David had
committed a terrible sin, a terrible crime. He was
guilty of murder, he was guilty of adultery, and yet
he went on as if he had done nothing at all. And he
had to be pulled up by the prophet Nathan, who
showed him what he had done and made him face
himself. It was then he realized what exactly he
had done. That is always the first step. If you are a
person who has not sat down and looked at himself,
whatever else is true of you, I can tell you that you
are not a Christian. It is impossible to be a
Christian without facing yourself and looking at

your own life. The world does its best to prevent us doing that. With its organized pleasures and all its suggestive attractions it is doing everything it can to prevent people sitting down and thinking and facing themselves and their own lives. But the man who is a Christian has passed all that. He has stopped and has looked, he has examined, he has recognized certain things about himself, he has made a certain confession. You will find that in the first verse of the psalm.

Then the second step is that a man who becomes a Christian is a man who has come to realize his own utter helplessness. He has come to realize his need of mercy, his need of forgiveness. He is the man who has said, 'Have mercy upon me, O God, according to thy lovingkindness; according unto the multitude of thy tender mercies blot out my transgressions.' He is a man who has come to see that he cannot get rid of the sense of guilt himself, he cannot find peace and rest for his heart and mind as the result of anything he does. In desperation he turns to God, the God whom he has offended, and says to himself, 'My only hope is in God. The only one who can give me peace is the one I have offended most of all.' So he casts himself upon that one's love and compassion and mercy.

And so the point at which we have arrived is that the man who does not realize that he needs forgiveness is not a Christian. You can call him a moral man if you like, call him an ethical person, call him anything you like. I do not deny he may be all those things; but I say a man literally cannot be a Christian unless he realizes he is a sinner and needs forgiveness and mercy and compassion from God, and cries out for it. It is one of those essential things without which one has no right whatsoever to the great and exalted name of Christian.

But you notice David did not stop there. He went beyond that. And I want to emphasize that every true Christian invariably and of necessity must always go beyond that point. The first thing a man becomes conscious of is the need of forgiveness. We all know something about an accusing, tormenting conscience, I am sure—the feeling that we have done wrong and that we want to get rid of that sense of guilt, that unhappiness. We want to feel at rest and at peace. That is the first thing the convicted sinner always feels. The man who has stopped and looked at himself and seen what he has done is a man who is unhappy and who wants to get out of that state of unhappiness. But the true Christian does not stop there. The next step is to see and to hate that terrible thing within us that ever makes us capable of sin.

You see these steps in the case of King David. First of all he is thoughtless. Then he is arrested, he sees his transgression and iniquity and sin. Then the feeling of guilt and the desire to be rid of this and the cry, 'Have mercy upon me, O God.' But he did not stop at that. He went further and he said, 'The terrible thing is this, that I was ever capable of that adultery and murder.' Now that is of the very essence of the Christian position. The Christian never stops merely at the desire to be forgiven; he always accuses and examines himself to such an extent that he becomes troubled and concerned more about the thing within him which renders him capable of such an action than the action itself. Forgiveness is no longer to him the great question; it is the thing within him that ever put him in the position of needing forgiveness. I trust I am making this plain and clear. I am afraid it is a very superficial evangelism which seems to stop at forgiveness as if that is the only problem. No, no, there is something more terrible than the need of forgiveness, it is that there is something in me that puts me in such a position that I need it. That is the position to which David advances, and that is the thing he expresses so poignantly in this tenth verse: 'Create in me a clean heart, O God.' 'That is my real trouble,' he seems to say, 'it is my heart that is wrong.' And here he is crying out for God—'God, create in me a clean heart.' This is something which is always present in every true Christian. He realizes his need of a new nature, he realizes the need of a rebirth—of regeneration. The true Christian is a man who realizes that it is not enough to be forgiven and to decide to live a better life; he comes to see that he must be made anew, that unless God does something in the depth of his being he is altogether lost. He realizes the need of being born again and being created anew.

Now that is the subject to which I am drawing your attention in this third study. It is a very great subject, a subject about which volumes have been written, and obviously I cannot pretend to deal with it exhaustively here. But I am going to show you the doctrine of regeneration as it is taught in the fifty-first psalm. It does not tell us everything about it. I am simply confining myself to the exposition of it that is given here by David in his agony and in his prayer.

However, let me say in passing that nothing, it seems to me, is quite so strange as the way in which man by nature always objects to this doctrine of regeneration. There is nothing also, I sometimes think, that so demonstrates the depth of sin in the human heart as this objection to the doctrine of the rebirth or being born again. Read the New Testament Scriptures and you will find that men objected to it in those days. When our Lord and Saviour Jesus Christ spoke about it, He was always persecuted. People disliked Him for mentioning it. When He began to expose the depth of iniquity in the human heart and to talk about a rebirth they invariably misunderstood Him. They disliked it then and it has always been the same ever since. When John Wesley was truly converted he went back to his university at Oxford and preached a sermon on this very subject; and he was hated for it. Those respectable religious people there in Oxford disliked this doctrine, and they made it impossible for him to continue preaching there. The natural man, the natural, unregenerate human heart, objected to this great and wondrous biblical doctrine of the rebirth and regeneration. And it is equally true today. People sit and listen to an address or sermon on what is called the fatherhood of God or the brotherhood of man and they never object to it. When they are exhorted to live a better life they never express any objection at all. They say it is perfectly right, and even though they are reprimanded for not living better lives, they say that it is perfectly true and quite fair and that they could be better. But if a preacher stands before the natural man and says, 'You must be born again— you must have a new life from God,' they ask, 'What is this strange doctrine?' I remember very well on one occasion I was preaching in the heart of England in a farming community, and I had the pleasure of being entertained by a farmer and his wife. I remember that evening at supper the farmer's wife began speaking of another farmer's wife and she said something like this: 'Yes, she is a very nice woman, a most excellent farmer's wife, and she is a very religious person; but, you know, she keeps on talking about being born again.' This good woman felt somehow or other that that was some kind of defect in the character of this other person. It was all right to be religious, but to keep talking about a new life and being born again was something she could not quite understand and she obviously regarded as almost a mental aberration.

Now that is a very common attitude. There is in the human heart by nature a rooted objection to the doctrine of the rebirth. What is the cause of it? It is not at all difficult to discover the answer to that question. When I am confronted by this doctrine, I deduce from it that I am in such a thoroughly bad state and condition that nothing less than being born again can put me right. And by nature I do not like that suggestion. The natural man is prepared to admit he is not one hundred per cent a saint; but if you tell him that he is absolutely rotten, and that not only is he not one hundred per cent a saint, but that unless he is born again he is hopeless, he will take umbrage and ask 'What are you suggesting?' He will feel that you are insulting him. Man as the result of sin and the Fall has certainly not lost his capacity to draw a right deduction from statements that are made; and that is precisely the implication of the doctrine of the rebirth. You remember how our Lord put it to Nicodemus, who went to Him one night.

Nicodemus said, 'Master, I have watched you, and observed your miracles, and have listened to you, and it is evident to me that you are a Teacher come from God, for no man could do these miracles except God be with him.' Then our Lord interrupted him and said, 'Except a man be born again, he cannot see the kingdom of God' (John 3:3). You remember the conversation that followed. Clearly Nicodemus's thought was something like this: 'I have been watching and listening to you, and I have come to the conclusion that you have something which I lack. I am a master in Israel, I have a good deal, but I am quite clear that you have more than I have. What have I to do in order to become like you?' Our Lord said to him, 'It is not a question of adding to what you have got; you must be born again, you have to go right back to the foundation— not addition, but regeneration.' But we do not like that, we do not by nature like a doctrine that tells us we are hopeless, that we are so sinful or rotten that we cannot be improved but must be literally created anew.

Or let me put it in this way. We object to the doctrine of the rebirth because it is a doctrine that tells us very clearly, by implication, that we really cannot put ourselves right. Now, there again is something to which the natural man always objects. That is why he never objects to an appeal which is made to him to live a better life. He rather likes that, for in a sense it is paying him a compliment. If I should say, 'Now this is the sort of life you ought to live, I appeal to you to rise to it', we would all by nature like it because I would be implying that we are capable of it. We always like a doctrine which suggests that we have the capacity. What the natural man dislikes is a doctrine that tells him that he can do nothing about it; that all his efforts and endeavours will land him nowhere; that he can fast and sweat and pray, but that he will find it to be as useless as Martin Luther did. He had been a monk fasting and praying in his cell, he had gone to Rome on a pilgrimage, and he had done everything a man could do to save himself, but he was as far away at the end as at the beginning. It cannot be done! But man by nature does not like that, and that is why we all fight against this doctrine of the rebirth which tells us at the outset that we can do nothing, that we must wait upon God and ask Him to do this for us.

Or let me put it in another way. These are the obvious explanations of the oppositition to the doctrine, but the real cause of the trouble is to be found at a deeper level. Why should I object when I am told in the gospel that I am so rotten that I must be born again? Why should I object when I am told that all my efforts and endeavours will not be adequate? Surely this is the answer: it is my failure to realize that I am face to face with God. We are so accustomed to looking at ourselves and to comparing ourselves with one another. We are all in competition with one another. Look at the professions, look at men in business; they are all vying with one another. Men say that you can only get on in this world by applying yourself—that is the whole idea of life which we have by nature; and we can satisfy one another and human standards up to a point. But in this matter which we are considering we are not concerned with man; we are face to face with God. David has already expressed it in the sixth verse: 'Behold, thou desirest truth in the inward parts.' If we realize for a moment that we are concerned with God and not with man, we very soon realize how lost we are and how helpless.

The other explanation, of course, is our failure to realize the truth about ourselves. David has already expressed that in the fifth verse: 'Behold, I was shapen in iniquity; and in sin did my mother conceive me.' A man who has realized that about himself does not object to a gospel which tells him he must be born again. It is the man who thinks that on the whole he is very good, and that the occasional black speck in his character can be removed very easily, who is opposed to this gospel. The man who sees he is shapen in iniquity and that in sin did his mother conceive him, when told that he is rotten and that he must be born again, says,

'I entirely agree. I know that my heart is in this rotten condition.'

There, then, are the reasons and explanations of this objection to the doctrine. But it is also true to say that it is a humiliating doctrine. Let us admit it, that no man by nature likes to be told he must be born again. It is true of all of us. Our ultimate trouble is our pride, our self-satisfaction, our self-esteem and our self-confidence. The gospel comes and deals a mortal blow to that self, and we do not like it. People have never liked it and they dislike it still. It is an uncomfortable and a humiliating doctrine, and yet it is of the very essence of the Christian position. It is all put perfectly in these two verses: 'Behold, thou desirest truth in the inward parts . . . Create in me a clean heart, O God' (verses 6 and 10).

Why must we be born again? That is the question. What is it that makes the rebirth an absolute necessity if we are truly to become Christian? The first answer is this—*the treachery and the insincerity of our natures*. David admits that in these words: 'Behold, thou desirest truth [or sincerity] in the inward parts.' That is the trouble. You see the steps through which David has gone. He has been examining himself, he has come to recognize his sins, the things he has done. Then he goes a step further and says, 'There is something rotten within me, within my heart, and in a sense I can do nothing about it, because I have come to see that I cannot trust myself. I lack sincerity in the depths of my very nature and being.' What a terrible confession for a man to make about himself! And yet it is something that every Christian must of necessity have come to see. Jeremiah put it in these words, 'The heart is deceitful above all things, and desperately wicked' (Jeremiah 17:9). A great saint put it in a hymn in these words,

I dare not trust the sweetest frame.

Do you trust yourself? If you do, you do not know yourself. Have you not yet discovered the twists and the turns and the perversion in your own heart? Have you not come to see the insincerity that is down in the centre? We are all hypocrites, we are all playing at make-believe, we are all pretending to be something we are not. Am I romancing or am I stating the simple truth? Should we all be perfectly happy if our imaginations and secret thoughts could be flashed on a screen for everybody to look at? No, these verses are perfectly true, and in that state and condition we are utterly helpless because we are concerned with God. We can pretend with one another, we can say we are sorry in order to be forgiven and yet not really mean it in our hearts, but the other person does not know. We want to get out of a difficulty, we want to avoid the pain, so we say we are sorry. But when we

◆

are dealing with God, all that is utterly useless. 'I am face to face with you, O God,' says David, 'and you desire truth and sincerity in the inward parts. I cannot get away from you.' 'The word of God', says the author of the Epistle to the Hebrews, 'is quick, and powerful, and sharper than any two-edged sword, piercing even to the dividing asunder of soul and spirit, and of the joints and marrow, and is a discerner of the thoughts and intents of the heart' and 'all things are naked and opened unto the eyes of him with whom we have to do' (Hebrews 4:12,13). Ah, if you are simply concerned about getting rid of your feeling of guilt and unhappiness and nothing more, I say you are not yet in the truly Christian position. The Christian goes further than that: he realizes this fundamental need of a central sincerity. He sees himself through the eyes of God. He knows he is being read as an open book, and whatever other people may see in him and think of him, he knows that God is reading the thoughts and intents of his heart and everything about him in the very recesses of his life. He knows that his nakedness is open to the eye of Almighty God.

But further, I know that I cannot make myself sincere. I resolve to be sincere, but I find I am still playing with myself, I fool myself. I keep my ledger with my profit and loss account and I am very successful in balancing my account. I am always on good terms with myself, I am an expert, to use the modern word, at rationalizing myself and my actions. I can explain what I do to myself, and it is all right for *me* to do it, though I condemn it in others. That is what I find about myself. I am not honest and sincere in the very centre of my life—but 'thou desirest truth in the inward parts'. And, try as I will, I am aware of this fundamental dishonesty, this insincerity down at the very centre of it all, and I cry out to God that He must do something about it. I see there the need of the rebirth. The thoughts and intents of my heart are of vital importance. I realize that there I am in a realm which I cannot control, and I fall back upon God and His omnipotence.

The second need of the rebirth I can put in this form. It is due to my *ignorance and lack of wisdom.* Listen again to verse 6: 'Behold, thou desirest truth in the inward parts: and in the hidden part thou shalt make me to know wisdom.' Oh! David knew his own heart so perfectly. You see the steps through which a man passes. First of all I have gone on heedlessly. I am then pulled up and arrested. Ah, yes, I say, I should not have done that. Then I go on to ask what made me do it and then I ask, How can it be put right? I am so insincere, I can do nothing. What can I do, then? I do not know what to do, I am helpless, I admit it. What do I need? 'Well,' said David, 'what I need above everything else is wisdom, I need light and illumination.

I confess quite frankly that as I try to handle my own case I come up against this blank wall. I cannot get right. I need some light from the outside.' Every Christian knows what I am talking about. You come to that desperate point at which you say, 'Well, what can I do? I cannot trust my own thoughts and ideas. I must have something outside myself. I need light to be thrown upon myself.' That is what these verses mean. David is crying out for wisdom in the hidden part. In other words, no man is truly a Christian until he realizes that human knowledge and wisdom and understanding are not enough; until he has come to see with Pascal, one of the greatest philosophers of all time, that the supreme achievement of reason is to bring a man to see the limits of reason and to make him cry out for revelation. I need wisdom. I need light. I need light upon my own heart. I am a very bad physician of myself because I know that I am not honest with myself. I do not face things squarely, I always want to defend myself, so I cannot treat myself. I need light on myself from the outside. I need more wisdom with respect to my true condition. I need light about holiness, how to live a holy life. I need light on God, I need the wisdom that I cannot provide for myself. I search but I cannot find it. I read biographies of the great men of the world who have not been Christian and I know that they have failed in life. They could not find happiness; I cannot find it.

◆

What can I do? I must ask God for it. Have you cried out for wisdom, have you sought for knowledge? If you have gotten to that point, then you are on the high road to salvation. Have you reached the stage of saying, 'I cannot think any more, I have thought until I cannot think any longer. What can I do? O God, cast light upon my condition!'? If you offer that prayer you will get the light. The man who cries out for this revelation and divine illumination never does so in vain. I need wisdom in the hidden part; I believe God can supply it.

But then, you see, David goes on to the next step. He realizes now, as the result of this wisdom that God has given him, that *he needs a clean heart, that he needs a new nature.* I need not keep you with this. There is a passage in the seventh chapter of the Gospel according to Mark that really puts the whole thing perfectly (Mark 7:14-23). 'Look,' said our Lord and Saviour Jesus Christ in effect to those people, 'do not blame your circumstances and conditions and surroundings for what you are. It is not that which goes in that defiles a man, it is that which comes out. You are paying attention to the washing of hands and the washing of the platters and things like that; you are blaming your difficult position, the things that are around and about you. You say, "I am in this filthy world and it takes me all my time to try to keep myself clean." 'No,' said Christ, 'that is not the trouble; the trouble is in your own heart. It is not that which enters in which defiles the man, it is that which comes out; it is out of the heart that come evil thoughts, murders, fornications, adulteries and all the evil things that he lusts after.' Now we all know that that in some shape or form is true of every one of us. The trouble is in us. You see how David came to that conclusion at long last; he has faced himself and he says, 'I am a murderer, I am an adulterer, I am rotten, I have been responsible for the death of innocent people—ah, the terrible question that confronts me is this, What made me do it? Was it Bathsheba or the other people? No, it is something foul and cankerous in me, in my heart, that made me lust. It is not what I see that is the trouble. It is this within me that makes me interpret things as I do. It is I myself—"Create in me a clean heart, O God."' Have you come to that position about yourself? Have you come to see that all your problems and difficulties arise from that central cause? That, I say, is something that happens to every true Christian. 'Behold, I was shapen in iniquity; and in sin did my mother conceive me.' The trouble with man is not that he does certain things that he should not do; it is that he ever has a heart to do them. It is this thing within us that makes us desire; though our conscience tells us that we should not do these things, yet we do them. That is

◆

the curse, this thing in the heart. We need a clean heart.

But David goes further: he realizes *he can never produce it*. He knows perfectly well that all the resolutions in the world can never change the heart. They can only control a man's actions up to a point. There is a value in the idea of New Year resolutions; as far as they go they may make you a better man. You can control your actions up to a point, but when you try to cleanse the heart, I assure you that the more you try, the blacker you will find it becomes. Read the lives of the saints and find how those wonderful men who tried to cleanse this foul heart always discovered increasing foulness, and at the end found it to be utterly hopeless. That was why David cried out with this great word, 'Create in me'—God alone can give me a clean heart, God alone can give me a new nature. 'My only hope', said David, 'is that He who created the world out of nothing and made man out of the dust of the earth and breathed into him the breath of life, will create within me a clean heart and give me a new nature.' That is the cry of the Old Testament. David had seen it in its essence, he had seen that that was his fundamental need. And the fundamental need of every man is an operation of God in the centre of life. O, do you know, my friend, that that is the very essence of the New Testament gospel and its wonderful message? Why did the Lord Jesus Christ

◆

come into this world? Why did He live, and die that death upon the cross and rise again? What is it all for? Was it that you and I might be forgiven and go on sinning, and then come back, and having lived somehow from sin to repentance and repentance to sin, just slink into heaven and avoid the punishment of hell and its terrible consequences? That is a blasphemous thought! He did it all, as Paul says in writing to Titus, 'that he might . . . purify unto himself a peculiar people, zealous of good works' (Titus 2:14). No, the glorious message of the gospel is not only that I am forgiven. Thank God, I am forgiven; the first statement is that my sins are blotted out like a thick cloud—God forgives me. But I am not satisfied with that. I do not want to go on sinning. I want to tackle this central problem. I want to live a life that is worthy. I want to get rid of this thing within me that makes me sin and makes me lust to sin. And this is the answer of the gospel—this wondrous doctrine of the rebirth and the new creation, being born again, becoming a partaker of the divine nature. The Son of God came down to earth and took upon Him human nature in order that He might start a new humanity, a new race of people to form a new kingdom. And what He does is this: to those who come to Him and realize they need a clean nature within themselves He gives His own nature. 'If any man be in Christ, he is a new creature: old things are passed away;

behold, all things are become new' (2 Corinthians 5:17). I should be very unhappy for anybody to think that the gospel tells men, 'Yes, God is love, and because God is love He has forgiven you in Jesus Christ. Very well, because of that, turn over a new leaf and start living a new life.' That would be to me a negation of the gospel. No, the gospel does not just forgive you and urge you to go back and live a better life. It gives a new life. It offers to make us sons of God, it offers to make us partakers of the divine nature. Its message is that God comes to dwell in us. As Paul puts it, 'I live; yet not I, but Christ liveth in me' (Galatians 2:20). You are not left to yourself, you are not sent back to the hopeless task of trying to improve yourself. God gives you a new life, a new start, a new beginning. You become a new man, you will find yourself in a new world with a new power and a new hope.

'Create in me a clean heart, O God.' Any man, I say, who offers that prayer with sincerity will always be answered. 'Ye must be born again,' said Jesus Christ; and a man who realizes that and who submits himself to Christ is born again. He has new life, the life of God in him; the centre of the trouble is cleansed by God, and he finds within himself a new outlook, a new power, a new hope, a new man.

Psalm 51:10-15

'Create in me a clean heart, O God;
and renew a right spirit within me. Cast me
not away from thy presence;
and take not thy holy spirit from me.
Restore unto me the joy of thy salvation;
and uphold me with thy free spirit.
Then will I teach transgressors thy ways;
and sinners shall be converted unto thee.
Deliver me from bloodguiltiness, O God, thou
God of my salvation: and my tongue
shall sing aloud of thy righteousness.
O Lord, open thou my lips
and my mouth shall shew forth thy praise'.

IV

DELIVERANCE AND NEW LIFE

◆

Psalm 51:10-15

◆

In our three previous studies we have seen that
this psalm is not only a classic statement of the biblical and Christian doctrine of repentance, and that
it shows us therefore in a very clear and dramatic
manner the various steps and stages in the process
of repentance, but that also, at one and the same
time, it reminds us in an equally striking manner
of some of the main characteristics of the true and
genuine Christian experience. Here in this Old
Testament psalm we have the cry of the human
heart that realizes its sinfulness in the presence of
God, the cry for the very things that are supplied
so gloriously and wondrously in the New

Testament gospel in and through our Lord and Saviour Jesus Christ.

Now I have been trying to trace with you the various steps and stages; and I have been careful to point out that we do not insist that all should experience these things in precisely the same order, or that there must be a kind of mechanical repetition of those essential elements in the Christian experience. Nevertheless we have been concerned to point out that there are certain things which are invariably present in a true Christian experience; and these are the steps we have detailed hitherto. First of all we saw that a man who is a Christian is a man who at some time or another has been awakened. He has come to himself and seen the horrible character of the things he has done. The next step, we saw, was that such a man always comes to realize his desperate need of forgiveness, and he turns back to the very God against whom he has sinned and casts himself entirely upon His mercy. And then we have considered how the third thing which has happened to the Christian is that he has seen his absolute need of rebirth and of a new nature. So that the doctrine of regeneration is to the true Christian one of the most glorious doctrines in the entire Bible. He praises God for that miracle of redemption.

Now we come to another characteristic of the true Christian, which is that he displays certain consequences that follow from everything that I have just been saying. There are certain inevitable consequences to those things—to a consciousness of sin as the result of the awakening, the need of forgiveness, and the prayer for the new nature. I want now to deal with those consequences, and as we do so, I would remind you once more of the principle I have been emphasizing each time, namely that what I am going to say is something that is found everywhere in the Bible. You notice the experience of the saints as given to us in the New Testament, and you will find they all conform to a fundamental pattern. Take any instance you like, they are all exactly the same. That is what is so wonderful in Scripture, that you find these same experiences repeated everywhere. Not only that, if you take up your hymn-book you will find that the hymn-writers who have had a genuine experience of the grace of God in Christ are saying the same thing again. It does not matter to what denomination they belong. The evangelical experience of the rebirth is the same in all countries and in all centuries, and that is why these great illustrations which we have in our hymns bear witness and testimony to the same things. Again, as you read the biographies of the saints throughout the running centuries you will find a repetition of the same experiences. Martin Luther, after he had painfully worked out for himself the essential doctrine of justification by faith only and the evangelical doctrine of redemption, then discovered that St Augustine had been saying the whole thing some eleven centuries before, and how surprised and amazed he was that he had been rediscovering what Augustine had already written! Many another saint has had the same experience. These things are absolutes, and therefore we must look at them very carefully.

Here, in other words, we have our only standard: it is not what you and I think that matters, it is what the Bible teaches. People have their own ideas as to what constitutes a Christian. You find, when you discuss these things with people, they say, 'What I say is this.' And because they say it, they think it must be true. But surely there is no ultimate final standard of what makes a man a Christian except this Book. What do we know of Christianity apart from this Book? What right have we to say, 'This is what I think makes a man a Christian?' Surely this Book is our only sanction and authority. We know nothing of Jesus Christ apart from what we find here, and we have no right to postulate what is the Christian experience apart from the teaching of God's Word. Here, I say, is the only test and the only standard. I would say again with Luther, 'I know no God save Jesus Christ.' I know nothing apart from what I find here, and what I find here is that I am passing through this world of time, and that I have got to meet God face to face, and that there is only one way in which I can do so without fear and horror and trembling and alarm and final destruction, and that is to give a ready obedience to what God tells me in His own Word, to believe on His Son the Lord Jesus Christ, and to surrender myself and my life to Him. If I do that, if I acknowledge my sin, if I realize my need of forgiveness and believe that I have it through Christ and His perfect work, if I plead and pray for this new birth and receive it, then I say there are certain things that are going to happen to me.

In other words, I mean that what I am about to say is a test. I can imagine nothing more terrible than for a man to go through a long life in this world assuming and imagining that he is a Christian, and then to find at the dread day of judgment that he has never been a Christian at all. These are the solemn words of Jesus Christ Himself: 'Many will say to me in that day, Lord, Lord, have we not prophesied in thy name? and in thy name have cast out devils? and in thy name done many wonderful works? And then will I profess unto them, I never knew you: depart from me, ye that work iniquity' (Matthew 7:22-23). To me (and that is why I am a preacher of this gospel) the most important thing for a man in this life and in this world is to know for certain that he is a Christian. It is the only place of safety, it is the only place of security, and in studying this psalm we

◆

have been showing certain tests which we can apply to ourselves. Here is the final test.

What are the consequences of repentance, faith in the Lord Jesus Christ and the rebirth? The first is *the possession of joy and of gladness*. You will notice how David puts it: 'Make me', he says in verse 8, 'to hear joy and gladness; that the bones which thou hast broken may rejoice.' But listen to him again as he puts it in the twelfth verse: '*Restore unto me the joy of thy salvation.*' He had known it, but he had lost it, and he wants to have it back. I say that any man who has gone through this experience of conversion, who is born again, is a man who knows this joy and gladness. Now let us be careful about this. There is a great deal of misunderstanding about this question of Christian joy. It is very important to note that the joy of which David speaks here, in exactly the same way as the Bible speaks of it everywhere else, is a particular joy. He is not talking about natural cheerfulness and joyfulness; he is not talking about something temperamental. The joy of which he speaks is what is called 'the joy of thy salvation'. It is a special joy. I am at pains to emphasize that for this reason. I am very willing to agree that temperamentally we differ tremendously one from another. There are some people who seem to be born with a kind of morbid, introspective, miserable and unhappy temperament, and there are other people who are born naturally cheerful, optimistic, bright. As you make an analysis of mankind from this psychological standpoint you will find there are all conceivable variations, from that thoroughly miserable, introspective type to this other kind of person who is always, as it were, jubilant and happy and rejoicing, whatever may be happening. Now the Bible is well aware of all that, of course, but its great message to us—and thank God for it!—is that the joy of which it speaks is entirely independent of all such natural conditions. It is the joy of God's salvation that is offered, and not some natural joy. Now that is important in this way: the biblical teaching is that every Christian ought to possess this joy, and that though you may be born naturally morbid you can still enjoy this particular joy.

One case, perhaps, will help to establish this point. I think that any psychologist will have to agree with me when I say that the apostle Paul was by birth and by nature a man who was given to morbidity and introspection; there was nothing of this naturally cheerful type of person about him. Yet there is no man who ever knew the joy of God's salvation more than the apostle Paul. Or take another case, a more modern one. Take a man like John Wesley. By no stretch of imagination can you think of John Wesley as a cheerful, happy type of individual. He was the very antithesis of that: scholarly, somewhat remote, with a kind of coldness in his very nature and make-up—temperamentally a naturally morbid man again. And yet he became a man who knew this great joy of salvation and gloried in it and rejoiced in it. I could take many other examples to establish the same point. What I say, therefore, is that if we are lacking in the joy of God's salvation, we cannot excuse ourselves on temperamental grounds and say, 'We are not all the same.' We are not discussing temperaments; we are discussing the joy of God's salvation which is offered to all, and which, according to the Bible, is meant for all. Take Peter, for instance, in his First Epistle (chapter 1, verse 8). He is writing to Christians and he wants them to rejoice, and he says to them, 'Though now ye see him not, yet believing, ye rejoice with joy unspeakable and full of glory'—all of them. He does not say, 'Some of you, the bright and the cheerful, are rejoicing in joy.' Not at all; all of us, everybody, every Christian.

So then, the question I ask is this. Do we know anything about this joy and gladness and rejoicing? I think I have established that it is something that is an inevitable consequence of the true, evangelical experience of the rebirth. But in case there is someone who is unhappy about this, and in my desire to be essentially practical, let me put it in this way. There are certain causes which tend to stand between people and the experience of this joy and gladness. Let me note some of them. The first,

◆

of course, is sin. That was the essence of David's trouble. 'Restore unto me', says David, 'the joy of thy salvation.' Why had he lost it? He had lost it because he was guilty of adultery and murder and the other things I have mentioned. My dear friend, there is no need to argue about this. Alas, we all of us know it painfully by experience. If we sin we break the communion and contact with God, and that always leads to misery and unhappiness. There are always conditions to God's blessings. We must love God; God calls us to love Him. I know many people who are living miserable Christian lives because they will not submit themselves to God. You cannot have it both ways. Read about the apostle Paul again and the amazing joy that he knew. Read the biographies of the saints and of their thrilling experiences. Why do we not all have that? It was not that they were special people. No, Paul says he is 'the chief of sinners'. How then did he know such joy? The essence of the secret is that he avoided sin, he lived the life to which God in Christ called him. Sin always robs of joy. Let us be careful about that.

But there is another reason also, and that is lack of understanding as to the way of salvation. There are many people who want to be Christian, there are many who would give the whole world if only they could have the joy that they read about in the Bible and in the lives of the saints. And yet they say, 'You know, I never seem to be able to get it. I have prayed and longed for it. The one thing I want is this great joy, and yet I never get it, it is always eluding me.' Well, sometimes, the cause for this is nothing but sheer ignorance or faulty teaching with respect to the way and the means of salvation. Without quite realizing it, these people are still trusting to themselves and to their own efforts. They have not realized that the gospel is as simple as this, that we have to come to God empty-handed, that we realize we can do nothing, that it is a gift from God which we receive. They are still trying to make themselves Christian, and as long as they do so they will never know the joy of salvation. Let me state it once more. It is just this—and how simple it is! We have all sinned against God. We can never get rid of our guilt, we can never remove the stain. My past remains and I cannot deal with it, and I fail in the present and shall fail in the future. How then can I meet God and be forgiven? Ah, the whole answer is that I can receive it as an immediate gift, that everything has been done in Christ, that Christ has died for my sin, and that because God has dealt with sin there, He offers me this free gift. Now there is the essence of this matter. You need not wait for anything; it is a gift that has to be received, just as you are and where you are at this moment.

Now there are many people who do not realize

this. They say, 'I must become a better man before I can say I am a Christian.' That is to deny the whole doctrine of forgiveness. The doctrine is that in sheer stark simplicity it is all given by God, in a moment, at once. He does not ask anything of us except to submit to Him. I hope there is no one going without the joy of salvation through a failure to realize that it is the free gift of God that can be taken at any moment. God does not ask you to do anything. He asks you to receive it now, to believe His word. Oh the tragedy that people should rob themselves of the joy for that reason!

Let me give you an example of this. That was the whole trouble with Luther. Luther was trying to make himself a Christian, and he was unhappy, as any man must be who tries to make himself a Christian, because it cannot be done. And then this blessed truth dawned upon him that these riches of God in Christ were a free gift and all he had to do was to receive them by faith. God had made him just in Christ. And in a moment all was well, and he began to rejoice. That also is the case with every other saint that the church has ever known.

A third reason which explains why many lack this joy of salvation is the simple reason that they spend too much time in looking at themselves instead of looking at the Lord. They set up for themselves a standard of perfection. I remember the sad case of a very godly man whom I knew who had two daughters who were most excellent women. They had reached middle life when I met them. They lived, in a sense, for the things of God, and yet neither of them had ever become a member of a Christian church, or ever taken communion at the Lord's table. As regards their life and conduct, you could not think of better people, and yet they had never become members of the church and they had never partaken of the bread and the wine. Why? They said they did not feel they were good enough. What was the matter with them? They were looking at themselves instead of at the finished, perfect work of Christ. You look at yourself and of course you will be miserable, for within there is blackness and darkness. The best saint when he looks at himself becomes unhappy; he sees things that should not be there, and if you and I spend our whole time looking at ourselves we shall remain in misery, and we shall lose the joy. Self-examination is all right, but introspection is bad. Let us draw the distinction between these two things. We can examine ourselves in the light of Scripture, and if we do that we shall be driven to Christ. But with introspection a man looks at himself and continues to do so, and refuses to be happy until he gets rid of the imperfections that are still there. Oh, the tragedy that we should spend our lives looking at ourselves instead of looking at Him who can set us free!

Is it not a wonderful thing that joy is at all possible to such creatures as we are? Is there not something almost daring about this prayer of David's? 'Restore unto me the joy of thy salvation,' says the adulterer and the murderer, the liar, the man who is responsible for so much trouble—'restore unto me the joy of thy salvation.' How can a man like that ever be happy? Is it possible? I thank God it is possible, and that is why I preach this gospel to you. That is the glory of this wonderful salvation. It can give this joy to a man who has sunk as low as that, and raise him to the heights of joy and gladness. And it does it like this. It can make even the worst sinner joyful and happy because it gives him an assurance of pardon and forgiveness. The only one who can pardon is God, and, thank God, He does so! And God not only pardons, He can make me know He has pardoned. To know that is to lose that miserable sense of guilt and frustration. Nobody else can do it, but God can do it. So, though I may have sunk to the lowest depths of sin and degradation, He can make me rejoice in His great salvation.

Then, of course, He does it by giving me a new nature and a sense of a new start and a new beginning. No man can ever be really joyful and happy if he feels he has to spend the rest of his life exactly as he was before, because he argues like this. He says, 'I am sorry I did that, and yet I go on doing the same thing again. Oh, wretched man that I am, what a miserable existence I find myself in!' But here is an offer of a new nature, a new start and beginning. That is the gospel of Jesus Christ. He offers to create us anew, to make us new men with the divine nature within us, and we have a new start in life. Not only that, but that in turn makes a man feel deliverance is really possible. 'I need Thee every hour,' says the Christian; 'stay Thou near by'. Why? 'Temptations lose their power, when Thou art nigh.' I begin to feel He is with me; and He is stronger than the devil. He has conquered the devil and can enable me to conquer.

Another way in which He enables me to joy and rejoice is that He enables me to forget my miserable, wretched self. That is one of the most wonderful things of all. You see, here is a man like David, and he has done these things. Now, if a man like that begins to look at himself he will be down in the depths of despair; but when God makes us look at Christ, He makes us look at His love and compassion and mercy. As you do so you get rid of self, you forget yourself—it is the only way I have known of forgetting self. The way to be happy, according to the gospel, is to look at the Lord Jesus Christ. You see that the Son of God came out of heaven to this world to die for your sins. You see Him there, by faith, in glory, looking upon you and waiting to shower His great light and power and strength upon you. And as you think of His love and compassion you forget yourself and the sin, and you begin to rejoice and praise Him. You have the joy of His great salvation. That is how it is done. Do you know the joy of God's salvation? Do you know what it is to rejoice in the Lord, to be joyful in Christ?

The second characteristic of the Christian is always this: *a profound distrust of self and a realization of the power of God*. Listen to David. He has already said, 'Create in me a clean heart . . . and renew a right spirit within me.' In the Revised Version margin it is put in this way—'Renew a *stedfast* spirit within me.' You see, what he was conscious of was his own unsteadiness. Well might David have felt that. He was a man who had experienced God's blessing, and he had known the joy of the Lord; and yet he had fallen into these terrible sins. So he cries out for this renewal and for this reliable spirit within himself. I make bold to say that every Christian knows what this means. A Christian is not a man who relies upon himself. It is only the Christian who knows his own weakness. It takes a Christian to see the blackness of his own heart and the frailty of his own nature. There is a type of Christian, I regret to say, who behaves as if he can do everything. He has had an experience of conversion, and now he is ready to face hell and the devil and everything. Poor fellow, he will not go

◆

very far before he loses that sense of confidence. 'Let him that thinketh he standeth', said the apostle Paul to such people, 'take heed lest he fall' (1 Corinthians 10:12). No, the Christian is a man who knows his own weakness, and he is afraid of it. So he prays for a steady spirit, a reliable spirit. He wants to be a sound man.

What else? Here is the next thing—'Restore unto me the joy of thy salvation; and uphold me.' 'Uphold me—I cannot hold myself,' he says. 'Hold me up, I am frail and weak, and the world is dark and sinful. I am surrounded by temptation and the insinuations and suggestions of sin. I am afraid I will fall; hold Thou me up.' That is the Christian— a man who realizes that unless God holds him up he will certainly fall. And the last thing he expresses here is this—'Restore unto me the joy of thy salvation; and uphold me', says the Authorized Version, 'with thy free spirit.' It is agreed that that is a wrong translation; it is better like this— 'uphold me with a willing spirit'. In other words, what he is praying for is this: 'I ask that Thou wilt fill me with a willing spirit, so that I shall always be willing for every request that Thou dost make of me. I want to be willing to run in the way of Thy commandments, so restore unto me this joy of Thy salvation and hold me up with a willing and right spirit.' And of course the Christian knows that all that is only possible in one way—the way that

David has already expressed in the words, 'Cast me not away from thy presence; and take not thy holy spirit from me.' That was his greatest fear of all, that God because of his sin might turn His back upon him. 'Don't do so,' cries David; 'don't cast me out of thy presence, take not thy holy spirit from me.' In other words, the Christian realizes this, that as he needs a steadiness in his life, as he needs to be upheld, and as he needs this willing spirit, there is only one answer, and it is the answer of the gift of the Holy Spirit. And, thank God, that is the answer of the New Testament gospel. God puts His Spirit into us; and the Spirit of God can make us steady, He can uphold us, He can give us this willingness, this readiness to run in the way of God's commandments. The Christian's confidence is never in himself; it is in the power of the Holy Ghost that God in Christ, and through Christ, has given to him.

The last thing I would mention is this. The last characteristic of the Christian is that he now *desires to live for the glory of God, and he is anxious that all others should do the same.* Listen to David in verses 13-15: 'Then will I teach transgressors thy ways; and sinners shall be converted unto thee. Deliver me from bloodguiltiness, O God, thou God of my salvation: and my tongue shall sing aloud of thy righteousness. O Lord, open thou my lips; and my mouth shall show forth thy praise.' I need not stay with this. Any man who realizes that God in His grace has forgiven him his sin, and has blotted out his transgressions, and cleansed and washed him; any man who realizes how vile he has been, and how wonderful this grace and life from God are—any man who has realized that and really experienced it must of necessity feel that there is only one thing to do in this life and this world, and that is to live to the glory of God. If a man does not feel that, he is despicable. If I stand here and say that I believe that God sent His only begotten Son to that cruel cross on Calvary to die for my sins, that God has loved me so much that He has done that for me— if I say that and I do not want to live to the honour and glory of God, I say I am the most ungrateful wretch that the world has ever seen. There is no need to argue about these things. If a man does you a kind action you feel a sense of gratitude towards him, and you say, 'Look here, is there anything I can do for you? If ever you find yourself in any trouble let me know. I feel that I owe so much to you, let me do what I can for you.' And here is the holy God who has forgiven us our foul sins even at the cost of the shed blood of His own Son! There should be no need to appeal to men to be holy: it should be enough just to tell them what God has done and then leave it to their sense of honour.

◆

'O God,' says David, 'restore unto me the joy of thy salvation; and uphold me with thy free spirit. *Then'*, inevitably, 'will I teach transgressors thy ways; and sinners shall be converted unto thee.' I will spend my time, he says, in telling forth Thy praise, in ministering to Thy glory. I will persuade others to come to Thee; I will look at them with a different eye. I will see them as I have been myself, missing the greatest and the most wonderful thing in life, and I will say to them, 'Come to God, face your sin, believe on Him, and you will get this amazing joy and the upholding and the strength and all you need.' *'Then'*—and it is this 'then', I say, which is inevitable in every true Christian. A Christian, in other words, is a man who realizes the truth about himself, and who has received so much from God that he wants everybody else to have the same thing. It is like a man who may have been suffering for years from some painful disease or illness, who has tried all the physicians of his own country and of other countries and found no cure, and at last stumbles upon a cure and finds relief and release. What does that man desire? He wants all other sufferers from the same disease to know about his cure. He feels he owes it to them. He sees a similar case and he says, 'Have you tried this? It has worked wonders in me. Oh that you might try it and become as I am!' And it is exactly the same with every true Christian. The man who is a

Christian is sorry for those who are dwelling in sin. He is sorry for this unhappy world trying to find joy and never getting it, trying to draw water from a broken cistern and never finding satisfaction. He sees men getting nearer to death and the end, to judgment and ultimate perdition, and he is unhappy about them. He sees them blinded by Satan, missing the most glorious thing of all, and he wants them to know it. So, having had it himself, he does his utmost that others may have it also.

Thus we have looked together at some of the characteristics of the Christian. My friend, I have said already, and I say it again, the most important question in the world is just that. Are you a Christian? Do you know anything of this joy? Do you know anything of this supreme confidence in the power of the Holy Spirit? Do you feel you have something that you would like others to have? Those are some of the simple tests. If you have it, may God continue to bless you. If you do not have it, if you feel that these simple tests have condemned you, and you feel you are not a Christian at all, then all I say is this: Go and confess it to God. Do not lose a moment. Tell Him that you have been misleading yourself, that you realize you are not a Christian. Tell Him you want to be a Christian, ask Him by His Holy Spirit to enlighten you. It is as simple as that—confess your sin, acknowledge your

———————◆———————

transgression and ask Him for this pardon in Christ; and you will receive it. Then thank Him, and go and tell others, who are in like darkness and in the same misery, about Him. Amen.